Don't Learn 4 Exams!

The Keys to Unlocking Your True Potential

Don't Learn 4 Exams!

10 Exam Secrets Of Highly Successful Teens

Laura Lyseight

Copyright © 2010 by Laura Lyseight.

Library of Congress Control Number:		2010901269
ISBN:	Hardcover	978-1-4500-3448-7
	Softcover	978-1-4500-3447-0
	E-book	978-1-4500-3449-4

All rights reserved. No part of this book may be reproduced or transmitted in any form or by any means, electronic or mechanical, including photocopying, recording, or by any information storage and retrieval system, without permission in writing from the copyright owner.

Visit www.successfulteens.co.uk
www.success4teens.info
www.lauralyseight.com

This book was printed in the United States of America.

To order additional copies of this book, contact:
Xlibris Corporation
1-888-795-4274
www.Xlibris.com
Orders@Xlibris.com

Contents

Foreword 9
Acknowledgement 11
Introduction 13

I	Reprogram Your Mind-Set 17
II	Tips 23
III	Physical Health 30
IV	Nutritional Health 35
V	Emotion 42
VI	Developing A Sharp Memory 49
VII	Know Your Learning Style 55
VIII	10 Practical Learning Steps 60
IX	Practical Examination Tips 64
X	Wise Sayings and Quotations 69

Conclusion: Success: A Pre-Meditated Act 71
Appendix 75
Mind Maps 77
Mnemonics 79

DEDICATION

To all my privately tutored students, who have a desire to be *simply the best*.

To all teens and students from all walks of life, who are motivated to be achievers, who possess within them an unquenchable desire to reach their destination of greatness.

To the millions of students with highly untapped minds and potential who my heart burns for, to realize their *true* purpose and dreams.

To the author and finisher of my faith—my creator.

Foreword

As someone who has benefited from education, I am always keen to stress the importance of exam success; it can pave the way for your future and set the tone for the rest of your lives as teens.

I would always encourage all people to aspire, to aim for a better life, to reach their full potential, to access opportunities available to them, and to do their very best!

While there are many routes to success, education is definitely a very important factor and I think it is important for young people to use the tools available to them. This is the kind of book that will help many young people including my own children gain success in their *exams*.

I wish you the best of luck in your exams!

Sir Robin Wales
Mayor of Newham

Acknowledgement

Thanks to my awesome God, for gifting me, with great ambition and drive.

Thanks to my parents, for giving me the best education, their unparalleled love and their prayers.

To my wonderful sisters, who have been supportive and caring.

I am indebted to my sweet husband Adrian, for being understanding, patient, and for showering me with all his love.

To Sandra, an intelligent, talented and promising young lady, for helping proofread this book.

I am deeply thankful to Olise and his family, whose help and advice on this book have been invaluable.

I am excited to have such a dynamic friend in my life—George Offei.

To Mrs. Ethelena Lyseight and Mr. Richard Mpopo, who took their time to help me maximize the potential of this book.

To all my students who motivated me to write this book.

Introduction

One of the greatest tragedies in your study life is finishing without realizing and using your full gifts, abilities, and talents. It is frustrating to see students settle for only a fraction of their true capabilities due to a lack of direction and misguided priorities.

This book will challenge, inspire, and motivate you to become an achiever who maximizes his true potential and learns the secrets of successful teens.

I have worked with many students who miss out on the main ingredient for success. They lack zeal, purpose, and ambition. It is very disheartening to see students going back and forth from school with no real aim, and their typical answer to "What did you achieve in school today?" is simply "Emmmm, nothing," or "I am not sure!"
You will agree with me that even though two teens may be equal in their short of a correct answer, the teen who replies "I'll find out" is more valuable to his family, teacher, friends, and to himself than to the teen who simply replies, "I don't know," and does not make any effort to find out.

There is a missing desire to rise above the status quo—to excel and to soar beyond their wildest dreams—and this book aims to help put a stop to that train of thought and attitude. It aims to reveal the attributes of success and the habits of teens destined for greatness.

The very silent outcry of most teens is not knowing how to juggle the changes they experience as adolescents—mood swings, boredom, and depression, which, unknown to them, are due to an influx of hormones. As a teen, you are normally not sure how to create a balance between school life, homework, friends, peer pressure, and parties, to say a few.

However, I can assure you not to worry, as this is very normal and everyone goes through this period in his life. Even your parents and teachers did, too.

You might want to argue that their era was nothing compared to these prevalent knife and gun culture times, the curse of the mobile phone (even though most of you will dispute that fact and call it a blessing), PlayStations, Nintendo, and iPods. Not leaving out the fashion trends that teens are being exposed to nowadays.

Nevertheless, in all of these uncertainties and chaotic experiences, remember that throughout your life, you are constantly building your future, and how you build it will determine how well you will live in the *near future*. The foundation you build *today* will hold you *tomorrow*. The same friends you are with *today* will want to know your achievements *tomorrow. Be wise!*

"Twenty years from now, you will be more disappointed by the things that you did not do than by the ones you did do."
Mark Twain

I would like you to analyze the story below and always remember it as you strive to be your very best.

A hardworking building contractor, who worked for a famous real estate development company, had finally come to the day of his retirement.

He took the last of his pictures off his office wall, and just then, heard a knock on his office door.

In stepped his senior manager. "Tom, have you got a minute?" he asked.

"Of course I do. Thanks for the farewell party, it was well-organized and I enjoyed myself," said Tom heartily.

"Well, Tom, we just got a new contract to build this lavish five-bedroom house with a luxury swimming pool, tennis court, and a gymnasium in the basement. In short, the finest facilities." Tom's senior manager said, showing Tom the floor plan of the building, "We want you to be the project manager for this contract. We are willing and prepared to pay you double once the project is completed. Sorry for the inconvenience, but we know it will be built with excellence and in record time with you as the project manager."

Tom was utterly surprised. He was speechless. He felt devastated and was very unprepared for this new proposal. However, he thought to himself, "I will complete this project, but I'll do it haphazardly and retire happily within a month or two." True to his word, he did just that.

On completion, Tom's bosses went around to inspect the finished project. He was then handed the keys to the supposedly lavish house and the senior manager said, "Tom this is the company's gift to you, for all your years of dedicated service, loyalty, and devotion." You can imagine the rest of this story.

The question now is, what if Tom had only built to the best of his ability? The same question goes to you. Are you learning to the best of your capabilities? Are you performing at your best? Remember, you are the one who will benefit in the long run, just like Tom. Be aware that you are not learning for your parents or teachers, even though it may look like it, as they are the ones who are probably hammering in the need for you to excel in your academics. Lay hold of this picture in your mind as you aspire to do extremely well. The key is to endeavor at all times to produce your very best.

Life is accumulative. Whatever you sow today, you will surely reap tomorrow. Keep sowing *seeds of success*, keep *learning*, keep *reading*, be the best you possibly can be.

Believe that you are gifted, talented, intelligent, and unique, and the accomplishments that you reap will ensure that you leave your own footprint on this planet. Do not settle for less. You are *simply* the *best*.

ONE

REPROGRAM YOUR MIND-SET

You need to have a *big* enough reason why you should make the grades you desire and deserve to generally be successful in life. Nonetheless, academics alone is not the only surest way to success in life, although it's a necessary stepping stone to great achievement.

The truth is that nobody wants to be a failure even if the only reason for going to school is the norm and status quo of the society in which they live.

We are all born winners, but the choice is entirely yours. To pursue failure or success is an option. The fact that you are here means you competed with millions of sperms and won the battle of being the *one* to fertilize the egg. That is why you are born to win. You fought a good fight to get here, why be a failure now?

Unveil the power of possibilities that lie within you. You are more than what meets the natural eye. You are designed for success.

> **"If we did the things we are capable of, we would astound ourselves".**
> Thomas Edison

You are actually endowed with the seeds of greatness!

Do you know that more minerals (gold, diamonds, silver, etc.) have been mined from the minds of men than has ever been mined from the earth? Tap into the hidden treasures of your mind. Your brain, believe it or not, is stronger than the most powerful computer ever manufactured.

As a rule, one question I ask all my students is "What is your reason for studying?" Note that the true reason why you learn is to make sure you are developing yourself and your brain, which is different from your body, because it does not cease to grow. *Your brain never stops growing*. Therefore, search for knowledge and understanding.

The amazing thing is, once you are exposed to new ideas, you will never shrink back to your original or former state of existence as Napoleon Hill Discovered. Search and pursue wisdom with all your might. Your search should not only be for excellent grades, but for developing your entire self.

Once you transform and change your *old thinking* about studying, the real reason why you need to study will unfold and you will be on your way to excellence.

There is a *diamond* inside your brain, polish it and it will begin to sparkle. Refine that *gold* buried in your mind to the benefit of all. The power of a trained brain cannot be underestimated, therefore, anything you envisage yourself achieving is achievable.

> **"Whatever your mind can conceive and believe, you can achieve."**
> Napoleon Hill

Aim high and the results will follow.

Do not imprison and immobilize your inherent and natural God-given ability. You have been deliberately made up.

There is an indescribable and unexplainable feeling that comes with achievement and success. Break the root of what is holding you back in mediocrity. Set a new record and experience it for yourself.

There's no telling what you can do or achieve if you just try.

Valuable advice—turn all your *zeroes* into *heroes*. *Do not let your zeroes get you down. Instead, change them to high marks.*

Study these famous quotes:

> **"Man is a product of his thoughts, what he thinks, he becomes."**
> Mahatma Gandhi

You will invariably become your thoughts.

> **"I know for sure that what we dwell on is who we become."**
> Oprah Winfrey

You will always become what you think about. So are you thinking success?

> **"The bitterness of studying is preferable to the bitterness of ignorance."**
> Unknown

It is better to go through the discipline of studying now than regretting it for the rest of your life.

> **"We should try to acquire knowledge from all the sources and by all means—studying the scriptures, contemplation, meditation, etc."**
> Rig Veda

Study from all areas of life.

> **"A person who won't read has no advantage over a person who can't read."**
> Mark Twain

You are no better than the uneducated if you do not read.

> **"Educating the mind without educating the heart is no education at all."**
> Aristotle

Let your learning have an effect on your life, let it transform your life.

> **"Don't just read the easy stuff. You may be entertained by it, but you will never grow from it."**
> Jim Rohn

Your mind is your most powerful asset and you rise and fall based on the rising and falling of your thoughts. Your thoughts have the power to make or break you, because whatever preoccupies your thoughts is what you will eventually become.

Your positive thoughts about your studies will result in you desiring to learn more, and the grades will no doubt follow. However, your negative thoughts will do the exact opposite. You see, your thoughts are always attracting or repelling things towards or away from you.

As you begin to change your mind-set through reprogramming your mental faculties, you are on the way to achievement. Train your mind to see all the possibilities of you acquiring your desired grades, your high expectations of coming out as the best and top of your class. That ability is inscribed in your genetic code so do not let the society in which you live tell you otherwise.

Feed your mind; nourish your imagination and let go of any negative thought. You are number one.

You are a success!

QUESTIONS THAT SUCCESSFUL TEENS ASK THEMSELVES

Write down four reasons why you need to study to be an achiever.

1. ....

....

2. ....

....

3. ....

....

4. ....

....

Write down practical ways in which you can change your mind-set.

....

....

....

What steps can you take to ensure that your studies become your top priority?

....

....

....

Send your answers to
laura.lyseight@successfulteens.co.uk for a gift.

Positive Affirmations of Highly Successful Teens

Today is a blessed day, a day of great opportunity, and *on* this day, I am an achiever.

I invest into my future by making an effort to study well and consistently.

I can be all that I am created to be by studying hard and to the best of my ability.

Two

TIPS

TIPS is an acronym for ***techniques, ideas, principles,*** **and** ***strategies***.

***T*—Techniques**: A series of methods for accomplishing a desired result. There are methods you can use to get the best results during your studies.

  i. Make your own revision notes. "*How?*" you may ask.

  ii. On A4 sheets you can simplify your notes by rewriting it with:

  - bullet points
  - mind maps
  - patterned notes
  - mnemonics

  These will be illustrated in the appendix.

  iii. Organize your notes carefully and neatly in a file.

  - Write a checklist of the topics that you want to revise for the day.
  - When you feel you have revised that topic well enough, give it a tick on your list.
  - At the end of the day you'll have a line of ticks, so you'll be able to see the progress you're making.
  - Reward yourself for progress.
  - Don't make your list too long. Remember that it's better to revise a small section and fully understand it, than to rush through a load of topics and not have the in-depth knowledge required.
  - Remember not to be too harsh on yourself if you fail to revise all of the topics on your list. Stay focused and organized.

I—**Ideas** : Make sure you capture the main idea of each topic on your revision notes. Note that a *shallow approach* to understanding an idea requires minimum effort, while a *deep approach* to understanding the same idea is striving to understand *that same* idea thoroughly. Deep-approach learning involves asking questions:

   a. What?
   b. Why?
   c. When?
   d. Where?
   e. How?
   f. What next?

Link your ideas in such a way that they are easy to remember. You can use funny stories, rhyming words, objects, and body parts to help develop a sharp and focused memory. Be creative in your ability to link ideas.

P—**Principles:** Generate the same results time and time again, no matter who, when, where, or how it is applied. Once you apply yourself to learning, success will inevitably follow. One of your principles should be to have a *disciplined, organized, and daily study time, fundamentally a routine.* Studies have shown that there's no substitute for regular daily study and learning of any kind becomes incredibly easy if you maintain a steady pace from start to finish.

"We are what we repeatedly do. Excellence, therefore, is not an act, but a habit."
Aristotle.

"Everyday, do something that will inch you closer to a better tomorrow."
Doug Firebaugh

"Either you run the day or the day runs."
Jim Rohn

Take control over your studies.

S—**Strategies:** A game plan to achieve the desired results. These strategies, once followed, will produce drastic and effective results.

   a. Write down the main points on each topic.

b. Read out loud or record on tape. Reason being you will listen to your own voice more than another's.
c. Cover the original revision file (the file we created under the ***Principle*** acronym).
d. Tell someone what you have learned. It could be either a parent, sibling, friend, colleague, or even a teacher. This will, no doubt, help boost your memory, your ability to share your ideas, and your confidence.

a. Remember to take thirty minutes of learning bites, with five—to ten-minute breaks. Your brain will absorb the information better this way, without you feeling exhausted and having days where you don't feel like learning. We will take a look at the acronym for tiredness, but before that, let's get finished with our strategies.
b. Repeat the above steps many times, and finally find questions to answer on your revised topic. Find questions from textbooks, the Internet, and past questions. You can also ask your teacher for past questions. The more questions you answer, the more familiar you become with exam-style questions.
c. Effectively organize your study

  i. Step-by-step
  ii. Lesson-by-lesson
  iii. Daily
  iv. Weekly
  v. Monthly
  vi. Short-term
  vii. Long-term

d. Practice; revise using flash cards and the drilling of basic math everyday.
e. Create your own timetable, paste it where you can easily see it, and follow it as best as you can. Make certain that within a week, you would have done some hours on each of the subjects, dedicating more hours to your most challenging subjects.

Apply these strategies over a period of time (at least three months), and you will see drastic improvement in your study life. The truth is that if you have not been getting your desired results, you simply may have repeatedly done a few wrong things or lacked the sound techniques, ideas, principles, and strategies discussed.

Mr. Rohn puts it this way:

"Failure is simply a few errors in judgement, repeated every day."
Jim Rohn

QUESTIONS THAT SUCCESSFUL TEENS ASK THEMSELVES

How can I cultivate a disciplined attitude towards my studies?

....

....

....

What will have to change to enable me form a disciplined and organized attitude towards my studies?

....

....

....

What habits have been preventing me from studying effectively?

....

....

....

How can I break these unproductive habits?

....

....

....

Send your answers to *laura.lyseight@successfulteens.co.uk* for a gift.

Positive Affirmations of Highly Successful Teens

I always study as if I have a test tomorrow.

I quit studying below my ability.

I have excellent techniques, ideas, plans, and strategies in place for my studies.

ACRONYM fOR TIREDNESS

T—Time is something tired people never get enough of.

I—Inwardly, they are not having as much fun in their study or in their life, as they should.

R—Ready to always admit they don't understand a topic being taught or anything being studied, without applying much effort.

E—Every little thing poses a problem and wears them out easily and completely.

D—Delay studying until the last minute when examinations are just around the corner. They are sometimes good starters but poor finishers.

N—Negativity and pessimism are their middle name, if not the first.

E—Extraordinary, they don't dream of becoming. Rather they become self-inflicted with mediocrity.

S—Success-oriented, they are not.

S—Strives for nothing, learns nothing, and becomes nothing.

I hope this acronym is not describing you.
It should not be a part of your character.

Three

PHYSICAL HEALTH

"A sound mind is found in a sound body." As the saying goes, your entire health determines your energy levels, which in turn has a great bearing on your ability to study effectively. The fact is that if you are not in a good state of health, your desire to even pick up a book will be a great chore.

Let's explore ways of ensuring tip-top physical health conditions.

Physical Exercise: The slightest form of movement in any part of the body helps to release tension. We are usually tensed-up unconsciously, and exercising should be a part of our daily routine, just as brushing of our teeth is.

A simple jogging exercise will send blood rushing to your brain cells, thus ensuring a fresh supply of oxygen to it. This will increase your ability to concentrate and absorb whatever information you need to study. These simple exercises that are going to be suggested can be done indoors or outdoors and can be done ten to fifteen minutes before you settle down to study.

1. Simple step-up and step-down exercise
2. Simple stretching exercises
3. Dancing with music
4. Running around
5. Jogging
6. Trampolining
7. Riding
8. Any movement that will send blood rushing to the brain and should be enjoyable and fun to do.

These simple activities will release some happy-feeling chemicals called serotonins. We can all do with a little bit of fun, since this is known to build the immune system, too. Once your immune system is strong, it will keep illnesses at bay and your learning ability high.

The whole idea here is not to overexercise, a maximum of fifteen minutes will do, so that you do not feel exhausted just before you start studying.

Studies with animals found that exercise increases brain concentrations. In a recent study, researchers found that adult mice doubled their number of new brain cells when they had access to running wheels.

Previous research also suggests that maintaining a healthy flow of blood and oxygen protects the brain. Running may in fact give the brain a workout. A new study found that individuals consistently scored higher on intellectual tests after embarking on a running program. Seniors at Duke University started a four-month exercise program. These seniors showed significant improvement in memory and other mental skills, also known as cognitive function.

Exercising makes us alert, and not stimulants such as coffee. Keep away from such stimulants, as they do not work well on the body in the long-term.

Exercise regularly and you will see positive results.

Secret Code for Teens who Exercise

E—Excited to move, shake, and make things happen.

X—X-tra energy levels.

E—Excel at all they do.

R—Repetition is the mother of all their skills.

C—Consistency is a major part of their lifestyle.

I—Intelligent, dynamic, and efficient in their endeavours.

S—Stress-free life is their ultimate aim.

E—Extend their knowledge in all areas of life.

QUESTIONS THAT SUCCESSFUL TEENS ASK THEMSELVES

Do I have a favorite exercise or exercises that I can perform just before I start to study? Write it down.

....

....

....

How many minutes am I willing to exercise before I start my study?

10 mins	....
15 mins	....
20 mins	....

How do I feel after exercising?

....

....

....

What is my level of absorption after exercising?

High	....
Moderate	....
Low	....

Send your answers to laura.lyseight@successfulteens.co.uk for a gift.

Positive Affirmations of Highly Successful Teens

I am in my best physical state of health, ready to move, shake, and study.

My mind is alert and ready to study, because of my perfect state of physical well-being.

My energy level knows no bounds.

Four

NUTRITIONAL HEALTH

Bear in mind that there is a significant link between *good nutrition* and a *powerful memory*.

> **"Nourish your mind like you would your body. The mind cannot survive on junk food."**
> Jim Rohn

Most of us do not nourish our *bodies* with the correct nutrition, let alone our *minds*.

Our overmodernized society has made life overtly simple and we are all reaping the repercussions.

Most ill health and a lack of drive in our lives are due to the overindulgence in one or more of the following eating habits:

1. Eating of food not conducive to good health.

    a) Fast food: Food prepared with excessive trans-fatty oils (oils that are not readily digestible). The effects of these oils will be explained in detail in later chapters.
    b) Overprocessed foods: for example, white bread, white rice, etc. These processed foods lack nutritional value. They have been overtampered with, so they can be cooked quickly and easily.
    c) Carbonated drinks (fizzies, soda, and pop) don't do our bodies a whole world of good. Admittedly, they do taste nice, but there is no telling the damage they cause to the body. Note that because you cannot physically cut yourself open or see the immediate results does not mean everything is alright.

    d) Sweets and crisps, as we all know, respectively have too much sugar and salt.

2. Nutrient-packed foods we should endeavor to consume:

    a) Whole, unprocessed foods like wholemeal breads, rice, nuts, and seeds.
    b) Cut down gradually on your intake of fast food.
    c) These unhealthy drinks (fizzies, soda, and pop) should gradually be replaced with drinking seven to eight glasses of fresh, distilled water.
    d) Instead of sweets, you could munch on some raisins (dried grapes).
    e) Eating a variety of fruits in season, we have been told by the National Health Service (NHS) that *five-a-day* could keep the doctor away.
    f) Lastly, make sure you combine your meals with lots of vegetables. They are packed with vitamins and minerals to help the digestive system function at its best. You do not want the kinds of food you eat to slow down your ability to study effectively.

Note that your brain is between seventy-five to ninety percent water, implying that dehydration will aggravate *poor memory and low attention span*.

WARNING: Don't wait until you are thirsty, by which time, it will be too late. Drink lots of the clear stuff and fluids.

"Take care of your body. It's the only place you have to live."
                      Jim Rohn

Some Beneficial Quotes On *Health*

"To insure good health; eat lightly, breathe deeply, live moderately, cultivate cheerfulness, and maintain an interest in life."
William Londen

"The higher your energy level, the more efficient your body. The more efficient your body, the better you feel, and the more you will use your talent to produce outstanding results."
Anthony Robbins

"Look to your health; and if you have it, praise God and value it next to conscience, for health is the second blessing that we mortals are capable of, a blessing money cannot buy."
Izaak Walton

"If you don't do what's best for your body, you're the one who comes up on the short end."
Julius Erving

QUESTIONS THAT SUCCESSFUL TEENS ASK THEMSELVES

Make a list of foods you need to put a stop to eating.

....

....

....

Which ones do I need to cut out gradually?

....

....

....

How can I make a conscious effort to drink between seven to eight glasses of water or fluids daily?

....

....

....

What reminders do I need to have in place in order to achieve the above results?

....

....

....

Send your answers to laura.lyseight@successfulteens.co.uk **for a gift**

MORE WISE SAYINGS—TO PONDER ON

"Wisdom is to the mind what health is to the body."
Francois de La Rochefoucauld

"A man too busy to take care of his own health is like a mechanic too busy to take care of his tools."
Spanish Proverb

"The wise man should consider that health is the greatest of human blessings. Let your medicine be your food and your food your medicine."
Hippocrates

"Those who think they have no time for healthy eating will sooner or later have to find time for illness."
Edward Stanley

Secret Code of Health-Conscious Teens

H—Happy at all times.

E—Energetic and vibrant.

A—Alert and alive.

L—Living life to the fullest.

T—Thinker, doer, and achiever.

H—High-spirited and optimistic at all times.

Positive Affirmations of Highly Successful Teens

I am healthy in every way, everyday.

To ensure super performance, I constantly put the right fuel in my body.

I have great fun eating and drinking healthily.

Five

EMOTION

The ability to be an achiever and go all-out in your studies or in life can be found in one single word: mind-set.

Know that your inner thoughts create your outer world. What you think of, you will no doubt become.

> **"Act as if you have already achieved your goal and it is yours."**
> Anthony Robbins

The only limitations we have as individuals are those we set up in our own minds. The good news is that we can take full charge of our emotions, thoughts, and feelings. They should not control us because we have total control over the way we feel.

> **"If you want your life to be more rewarding, you have to change the way you think."**
> Oprah Winfrey

Let's face a fact, if you are bored with your study life or with life in general, it means that you normally do not wake up with a burning desire to do things, to excel, and to perform at your best. In short, you may have no goals, no visions, no aspirations, and no passion for life. Well, somebody might say, "I have a vision to do well in my studies or in my life," yet they take no action and they study without any strategies in place.

Note, that *vision without action is fantasy, and mere action without vision is disorder.*

Hope your study is not disorderly and chaotic, because you have a clear mental picture of where you want to get to in life.

If you, however, feel sometimes that you are an underachiever, then shake that feeling off. You can achieve the very grades you want to come up with. Have learning strategies in place because doing that will help ease some of your emotional worries. There are also times when you don't feel like picking up your book to study, but that is alright as it happens to all, even the ones who always score the highest in your class.

The only danger in letting your feelings dictate you so often is that you might form a bad studying habit. Do not study only when you feel like it, because those feelings will rarely occur. The most natural feeling you will experience often is the feeling of tiredness and laziness towards your studies. Therefore, if you are a student who always listens to how you feel, then you know what destiny you are creating for yourself.

If there is a very important suggestion I want to leave with you on the subject of emotions, it will be that *you should learn to control your emotions, or else, they will certainly control you.* Learn to have balanced emotions about your studies. It will help you reach for the stars.

Be curious about how far you can stretch your mind, how long you can study for, and how well you can remember what you have learned. As you begin to experience success in your study life, you will feel the urge to study more, and the more strategic study you indulge in, the more success will follow. Soon a cycle of success will chase you down.

> **"The sign of intelligent people is their ability to control their emotions by the application of reason."**
> Marva Mannes

> **"Just as your car runs more smoothly and requires less energy to go faster and farther when the wheels are in perfect alignment, you perform better when your thoughts, feelings, emotions, goals, and values are in balance."**
> Brian Tracy

> **"It is the mind which creates the world around us, and even though we stand side by side in the same meadow, my eyes will never see what is beheld by yours, my heart will never stir to the emotions with which yours is touched."**
> George Gissing

> "The first and simplest emotion which we discover in the human mind is curiosity."
> Edmund Burke

> "Emotion always has its roots in the unconscious, and manifests itself in the body."
> Irene Claremont de Castillejo

Do not dwell only on your emotions, especially the negative ones, because they do not stand to good reasoning.

SPIRITUAL LEARNING

You must believe that your creator designed you to succeed in life. Therefore, you must strive to be all you can be in every aspect of your life.

Society will let you get by with little, but bear in mind that *mediocrity is self-inflicted, whereas genius is self-bestowed.*

Be the genius you were intended and designed to be. You are created in the image of God, so begin to speak and act like him. You are a creative genius and the whole universe will back you up once you aspire to succeed and be your best.
Be ready at all times, to ask the Master Creator for direction in all you do.

ASK Him for wisdom, knowledge, and intelligence.

Learn the acronym that successful teens know about *ASK*.

A—Ask
S—Seek
K—Knock

Let us analyze each of these letters.

A—Ask means to *make a request.* This is a simple act that does not require a lot of effort. We normally ask questions with our mouth, which is very easy, because you only have to speak it out.

S—Seek means to *go in search of or try to discover something.* This obviously requires more effort than asking. Here, instead of just placing a request, you actually go in pursuit of what you want. You might have to go hunting for what you are looking for.

K—Knock means to *strike or hit with a hard blow.* This act supersedes the above two and requires you to put in tremendous effort. A lot of energy is required.

This goes to show that if at first you do not succeed, then *try, try again.* There's absolutely no room for failures today!

Every human possesses the innate ability to push himself beyond every limitation and impediment set before him.

Do not accept any barriers put up to stop you realizing your God—given potential. Rediscover, redefine, release your talents and walk in your full capacity and potential.

Learn to develop a positive emotion towards your studies. When the word "studying" is mentioned, what emotion does it invoke in you? Hope it does not send shivers down your spine, but makes you feel something pleasant, because studies have proven that pleasant emotions appear to fade more slowly from our memory than unpleasant ones.

These are a few discoveries made about emotions:

- *Emotionally charged events are remembered better.*
- *Pleasant emotions are usually better-remembered than unpleasant ones.*
- *Positive memories contain more contextual details, which help build a strong memory.*

Based on this knowledge, make sure your study times are charged with excitement, and make learning as much fun as possible.

Also, your mood during your studies will reflect on your performance. Your emotional state of mind is vital to what you are able to absorb and recount during your studies. There has been quite a lot of research on the effect of mood on memory. It is clear that mood affects what is noticed and encoded in the mind.

Try to be in a good mood—especially during your studies—and arouse your senses. I'm talking about burning some essential oils during studying times or playing soft music in the background in chapter nine. Also, experiment to find out what works best for you. Add some stimulation, thrill, and enthusiasm to your studies.

Which is easier and fun to remember: the lyrics to your favorite song or giving a speech? It is easier to remember the song, and the reason being that you probably enjoy singing it, and you are most likely in a good mood when singing. You can always change anything that is hard to remember into the tune of a song and sing it. Sing it as many times as you can.

QUESTIONS THAT SUCCESSFUL TEENS ASK THEMSELVES

What are my feelings towards studying?

....

....

....

How can I develop positive feelings towards my studies and make studying fun?

....

....

....

How can I learn to focus on the outcome I want with my studies and not just dwell on my feelings?

....

....

....

Send your answers to laura.lyseight@successfulteens.co.uk for a gift.

Positive Affirmations of Highly Successful Teens

I have emotional balance towards my studies.

I always feel great after studying.

Studying is my way of life.

Six

DEVELOPING A SHARP MEMORY

All the previous chapters are geared towards developing a sharp and focused memory.

As we all know, physical activities keep our bodies strong and fit. Likewise. mental activities keep the mind *sharp, agile,* and *focused.*

An active brain produces new connections between nerve cells that allow communication with each other, ensuring a strong link between ideas, and thus resulting in a laser-focused memory.

The mind uses *energy* to store memory in a *specific location* and even more so, *more energy* is required to learn well, so as to be able to reproduce learned information effectively if need be, especially for examination.

The amount of energy stored with each memory determines how *fast* and how *well* you are able to recall it effortlessly and readily. What you need to understand on the other hand is that there are things that can cause *memory blockages*. This will be discussed later, but first, let's discuss ways to challenge yourself towards a better memory.

- Learn a new language.
- Learn a new hobby.
- Learn to play new games, example chess, Sudoku, and jigsaw puzzles.
- Read classic books (the Bible), because these are more challenging than popular books.
- Listen to classical music: Mozart, Beethoven, etc.
- Go to Google scholar to read academic papers.

Studies have shown that 50% of brainpower and function is genetic and 50% is environmentally acquired.

This is a good revelation since most people think that their IQ (intelligence quotient) is mainly genetic, and they like to blame their poor memory on generations before them. Based on this awareness, you can train yourself to be the finest, the best, the unbeatable in whatever you do.

Acknowledge the fact that nobody learns in isolation or from one source. Every experience and interaction with others adds to learning, knowledge, and wisdom. Based on this, you have the ability to filter out unnecessary information. This will help increase your memory capacity. Your memory capacity can be greatly expanded just by regularly cleansing your mind and thoughts.

From the above, we can clearly begin to understand why the majority of student populations have a poor or weak memory. A *poor memory* is the result of an *overloaded or preoccupied* mind. This is the natural state of mind of most teens. Their concentration is often divided between wanting to have the right clothes, hairstyles, latest fashion trend in town. an infatuation on the opposite sex, right down to mood swings, arguments with parents, a lack of confidence, and a struggle with peer pressure.

The best way to increase your memory capacity is by *decluttering* the brain of useless information. This action will increase your memory space and bank.

Imagine what happens when your computer is infected with cyber space contamination, it becomes really slow in responding to any command. This can be likened to a brain cluttered with a lot of unnecessary information. You need to change the software that makes your brain sluggish. **Stay focused!**

Let's now discuss what causes memory blockages. Let's look at the effect of nutrition; this is what I call the *food-brain connection*. Your diet affects the brain chemicals that influence your *mood and behavior,* your thought processes and *emotional reactions that ultimately create the story of your life.*

The working s*urface of your brain is made from fatty acids.* The good fatty acid that the brain needs are the Essential Fatty Acids (EFA).

An oleic acid is monounsaturated and can be found in extra virgin olive oil, almonds, pecans, macadamias, peanuts, and avocados. These are brilliant sources of the kind of oil the brain needs to function at its best.

However, the kind of oils that we normally eat are partially *hydrogenated vegetable* oils, which are a major source of unnatural fats highly detrimental to the brain cells. Modern food processing techniques have actually altered the basic building blocks of the brain. Trans-fatty acids are found in foods like *French fries, margarine, potato chips, etc*. Any partially hydrogenated oil will disrupt communication in your brain *slowly but surely*. Trans-fatty acids are rarely found in nature and are mostly man-made. Try to stay away from such.

The brain can be compared and likened to an unstable building that gets demolished during an earthquake, just as these modified natural fats alter the building blocks of the brain, thus weakening the brain structure and architecture.

This also gives rise to *stress*, a common trend of modern society.

FOODS THAT HAVE BEEN KNOWN TO BOOST THE BRAIN CELLS AND GIVE SHARP MEMORY

Avocado—are very rich in the essential fatty acids for the brain.

Blueberries—buy these fruits when they are in season. They produce and contain high levels of antioxidants, renewing and reviving the brain cells.

Wild salmon—the oils (omega-3 fatty acids) help to improve the brain's alertness and cognition.

Nuts and seeds—rich in beneficial fats. Contain plenty of vitamin E for cognitive function of the brain and protein. Examples are sunflower seeds, sesame seeds, macadamia nuts, and flax seeds.

Brown rice—has low glycemic index which is better for brain functioning and circulation.

Tomatoes—contain lycopene, an antioxidant particularly good for brain function.

Chocolate—I bet this has brought a smile to your face. Dark chocolate is rich in antioxidants and stimulates dopamine, one of the feel good receptors in the brain as well as releases serotonins.

A change in your diet to include the following will help your taste buds develop a natural appetite for them.

Would it not be great when you start eating the right kinds of foods for excellent brain functioning? Indulge in these natural foods and avoid the double burgers and fast food. Eat these sparingly and treat yourself to the right nutrition for your brain's sake.

QUESTIONS THAT SUCCESSFUL TEENS ASK THEMSELVES

Have I been feeding my brain correctly? Yes or no?
What have I been feeding my brain with?

....

....

....

How well can I begin to feed my brain and with what kind of food? Make a list of healthy food you can access easily.

....

....

....

What foods, rich in essential fatty acids should I begin to buy and make a part of my diet?

....

....

....

Send your answers to laura.lyseight@successfulteens.co.uk for a gift.

Positive Affirmations of Highly Successful Teens

I feed my brain with the necessary oils.

My brain functions to the best of its ability.

I have the brain of a genius; I have Einstein's brain.

Would it not be pathetic, sad and highly unacceptable to have an Albert Einstein's brain, but unknowingly settling for less, getting poor grades, and having a lack of ambition and drive to be an achiever like him.

Seven

KNOW YOUR LEARNING STYLE

There are three main ways we all learn and absorb information. There could be other ways, but I will discuss the three major ones.

1. *Photographic/Visual Learners*: People with this kind of memory are considered to have better-quality memories. These learners have the ability to recall, recollect, and replay images on the screen of their minds. Their minds are wired and designed to recall information better in the forms of images rather than in words. Let's take for instance somebody shouting the words "hot air balloon." People straight away see a picture of a hot air balloon floating in air, rather than the letters **h.o.t.a.i.r.b.a.l.l.o.o.n.** It is interesting to know that when we are young we often have the ability to recall vivid images and exercise our imagination, but gradually, in our teenage years, we lose this faculty as our minds become focused on the world around us and we drop this natural creative and imaginative ability.

Photographic/visual learners benefit from information in the forms of:

- o Diagrams
- o Charts
- o Maps
- o Pictures
- o Films, movies, or videos
- o Written directions

They also value to-do lists, assignment logs, and written notes. Interestingly enough, developing a photographic memory is something anyone can do for himself or herself.

2. *Kinesthetic or Hands-On Learners*: Learn best by moving parts of the body, activating their large or small muscles. They are known to think on their feet,

and using their hands frequently, etc. They learn often by wiggling, tapping, and moving their feet or legs, or basically any part of the body. Often, these learners are well coordinated and have a strong sense of timing and body movement.

They love to touch, feel, and experience the material at hand. It is amazing how most of us enter school during childhood as kinesthetic or tactual learners, running around, pushing, pulling, rolling, etc. Majority of people are kinesthetic learners, thus education is being geared to and is shifting towards a hands-on approach, thanks to this new awareness.

These groups of learners benefit from

- o Laboratory-based experiments
- o Technology
- o Arts and crafts
- o Dance
- o Drama
- o Basically anything involved with movement

3. *Auditory Learners*: Learn best by hearing information spoken or explained orally. They greatly benefit from traditional teaching techniques, speeches, forums, and lectures. They have strong language skills—which include a well-developed vocabulary—and greatly have an appreciation of words. They are usually good at carrying interesting conversations, and they speak intelligently. They are often talented musically and hear tunes and rhythms with precision.

Auditory learners benefit greatly from information in the form of:

- o Listening to lectures
- o A tape on class lecture notes
- o Discussing in small or large groups
- o Summarizing what they have read on tape
- o Verbally reviewing spelling words or lectures with another

Research has shown that some people learn through a combination of all three or more. However, every person has one primary learning program. Once you have discovered your style, you can then maximize it and efficiently use it to your benefit.

I totally agree with Henry who reckons:

> **"They know enough, who know how to study."**
> Henry Brook Adams

You are a success!

QUESTIONS THAT SUCCESSFUL TEENS ASK THEMSELVES

What is my learning style?

....

....

....

How can I use my learning style to the best of my ability?

....

....

....

How will this learning style help me to remember what I have learned?

....

....

....

What steps do I need to take to make my learning style most beneficial to me?

....

....

....

Send your answers to
laura.lyseight@successfulteens.co.uk for a gift.

Positive Affirmations of Highly Successful Teens

I am a photographic or an auditory or a kinesthetic learner.

I use my learning style to the best of my ability.

I get the best results from studies using my learning style.

Eight

10 PRACTICAL LEARNING STEPS

One problem or challenge most students say they face during examinations are either going blank or forgetting an answer in the middle of answering a question. Some even forget to spell a simple word such as *the*. This actually happened to me once, as well, when I was writing an exam. What is truly happening is *stress or anxiety. Let me try to explain it further. Blood is diverted to the back of the brain, instead of the forebrain.* You need the blood rushing to your forebrain so you can be alert and awake. When the blood is sent to the back of brain it does not aid your memory. When experiencing this void, there is *one* simple step you can take: you need *to breathe in more oxygen*.

During your time of study

- Ensure there is a constant supply of fresh air.
- The room should be bright and flooded with natural or artificial light.
- Ensure a good seating position and posture.
- A serene and quiet atmosphere.
- Have a potted plant to supply you with more oxygen.
- You can have soft music playing in the background. (Listening to a piece of Mozart music for ten minutes is known to improve the Intelligence Quotient—IQ.)
- Take short breaks.
- Know your absorption rate and which time of the day you are able to retain information the most and easily.
- Note that sleep and relaxation are needed for rejuvenation.
- Be optimistic at all times when studying, as this will send positive vibrations to the brain cells.
- Create a positive air around you.

These two quotes remind me about the necessity of rest, hope you learn from it too.

> "Learn to relax. Your body is precious, as it houses your mind and spirit. Inner peace begins with a relaxed body."
> Norman Vincent Peale

> "A good rest is half the work."
> Proverb

Your overall ability to get maximum results and retention of the material being studied has a lot to do with the above points. Most of these are subtle and may seem insignificant, but by just disciplining yourself and finding what works best for you could produce radical results in your studies.

Some students might say it is too late now, I should have known about this earlier when I was writing my SAT exams, 'O' level exams or 'A' level exams. It is never too late to start practicing. Listen to Teddy:

> "Do what you can, with what you have, where you are."
> Teddy Roosevelt

I understand what Mr. Howe says:

> "People are always neglecting something they can do and try to do something they cannot."
> Ed Howe

These steps, as simple as they may seem, will without a shadow of doubt transform and improve your studying times.

I enjoy this poem that talks about finding good information and using it immediately.

> "No longer forward nor behind I look in hope
> or fear; but grateful, take the good
> I find, the best of now and here."
> John Greenleaf Whittier

Do you know that the amount of studying success you achieve is totally dependent on your own devised effective plan and strategy? Your own ingenuity and resourcefulness is what will get you through hard and turbulent times. These are times when you do not feel like studying or times when you simply feel like doing something seemingly useless, so far as your academic success is concerned.

QUESTIONS THAT SUCCESSFUL TEENS ASK THEMSELVES

Have I made my study area into an environment that motivates me to learn? Yes or No?

How can I make my place of study so it will make me look forward to my studies?

....

....

....

Is my study area free from clutter?

Yes ....
No ....

If no, how can I get it organized and how can I develop a habit of keeping it clean at all times?

....

....

....

What things can I put in place to enhance my mood for studying?

....

....

....

Send your answers to laura.lyseight@successfulteens.co.uk for a gift.

Daily Affirmations of Highly Successful Teens

My study area is very inviting for studies.

It is never too late to put in my best effort.

My academic success is my priority at this point in my life.

Nine

PRACTICAL EXAMINATION TIPS

During an examination or test, the brain is put on the spot to remember all sorts of information, also to function at its optimum; it will require more nutrients than its norm.

The human brain on average weighs 1.5 kg, which is about the same size as a hefty and sturdy textbook. Thus we need to put into our bodies the nutrients that will feed and nourish the brain to aid its highest performance. Remember all the nuts and fish oils—natural source of the Essential Fatty Acids (EFAs), as well as fresh fruits, that were discussed earlier.

How to study effectively two months prior to examination date

Do you know that a high percentage of the material or information that you study just stays in your *short-term memory* and gets lost before it reaches our *long-term memory*? It is *almost* impossible to retain everything we read, learn, or hear for the first time, so repetition is key to your long-term memory. Never leave your revision till last minute, as is the practice of most students.

A good piece of advice: to reach long-term memory quickly and easily, note that when you come across a new *term, a date, an event or specific information* that seems as something you are likely to be tested on, jot it down on a flash card and review it as many times as possible (frequently and regularly). Here are some great times to review these cards.

- When an infomercial comes up while watching TV.
- Free time or period during school lessons.
- While visiting the toilet.
- When standing or sitting idly.
- Just before bed or whilst in bed.
- After a game on your PlayStation
- Basically any spare time, so you cut down on time wastage.

These cards should be with you at all times. Your sure passport to long-term memory!

A study has shown that scents can also help the brain to unlock memory. The burning of some oil-rosemary, lavender, peppermint and others—can help the brain achieve a better memory. It has been shown that if you wear the same scent during an examination as you wore during studying, you stand a better chance to perform better than others who did not. These oils can also be used during bath times to stimulate and energize the brain.

WHAT TO EAT DURING THE EXAMINATION DAY FOR HIGH AND LONG CONCENTRATION

- o Eat a meal that includes protein and is low in refined sugar. Try some eggs or fat-free cottage cheese.
- o Have wholemeal bread or porridge (oats), these have a low glycemic index, meaning, they release their energy slowly and prevent you from feeling hungry quickly.
- o Eat some banana, since this also has a low glycemic index.
- o For lunch you might want to try a sandwich with protein like turkey, chicken, salmon, or tuna.
- o Have a bottle of distilled water with you and take sips—not too much to prevent visiting the toilet unnecessarily.

RIGHT MOOD JUST BEFORE THE EXAMINATION

- o Calm yourself down by taking in deep breaths through your nose and breathing out through the mouth.
- o Make sure you have a good night's sleep the previous night and try not to study late into the night. This will confuse your short-term memory and leave you feeling blank the next morning.
- o Have an early night's sleep and wake up early, feeling rejuvenated.
- o Be optimistic and awake with a cheerful smile on your face. It does not matter whether you have finished revising or not. Lay hold of the thought that you are born a winner and victor.
- o Command the air around you to be positive.
- o Look over your flash cards for a quick reminder just before you settle in for the exam.
- o Make it a point to be on time for the exam.

CONSIDER THESE EXCELLENT STRATEGIES FOR ANSWERING QUESTIONS.

- o Read all instructions and questions very carefully.
- o Put a mark on questions you are not sure of, with the aim of coming back to try again.
- o Take your time and do not rush as this might lead to nervousness.
- o Do not focus your attention on the clock.
- o Do not let people who have seemingly finished early make you nervous or be a threat to you.
- o Make time to read over your work.
- o When in a dilemma between two answers, mostly choose the answer that came to you in the first instance.

QUESTIONS THAT SUCCESSFUL TEENS ASK THEMSELVES

Make a list of all the things you can do to help with your long-term memory two months prior to your exams.

....

....

....

Have I revised effectively for the individual subjects I am going to be tested on? If not, how can I encourage myself in these last few days to do my best?

....

....

....

Am I confident to score my desired mark? Write down what you think you will score based on your preparation.

....

....

....

How can make sure I have the right frame of mind during my exam?

....

....

Send your answers to laura.lyseight@successfulteens.co.uk for a gift.

Daily Affirmations of Highly Successful Teens

I am excited about my up-and-coming exams, because I am well-prepared.

I am ready to be tested on all I have learned.

I am in my right frame if mind and confident to get my desired results.

Ten

WISE SAYINGS AND QUOTATIONS

"Education is the most powerful weapon which you can use to change the world."
Nelson Mandela

"A goal is a dream with a deadline."
Napoleon Hill

"If I have seen farther than others, it is because I was standing on the shoulders of giants."
Isaac Newton

"The whole point of being alive is to evolve into the complete person you were intended to be."
Oprah Winfrey

"Success means having the courage, the determination, and the will to become the person you believe you were meant to be".
George Sheehan

"The first step toward success is taken when you refuse to be captive of the environment in which you first find yourself."
Mark Caine

"You must take personal responsibility. You cannot change the circumstances, the seasons, or the wind, but you can change yourself. That is something you have charge of."
Jim Rohn

"The difference between school and life. In school, you are taught a lesson and then given a test. In life you are given a test that teaches you a lesson."
Tom Bodett

"To do something, however small, to make others happier and better is the highest ambition, the most elevating hope, which can inspire a human being."
John Lubbock

"If you want to achieve excellence, you can get there today. As of this second, quit doing less-than-excellent work."
Thomas J. Watson

"Will you look back in life and say, "I wish I had or I am glad I did?"
Zig Ziglar

"There is always a way—if you are committed."
Anthony Robbins

"It is not enough to learn; one must believe, then become."
Fran Anne Briggs

"The will to win, the desire to succeed, the urge to reach your full potential... These are the keys that will unlock the door to personal excellence."
Eddie Robinson

"Education comes from within; you get it by struggle and effort and thought."
Napoleon Hill

"Anything I can do, you can do also and even greater things thereof."
Jesus

Conclusion

SUCCESS: A PRE-MEDITATED ACT

Our brains are completely reprogrammable. Whatever is programmed in your brain will set the limits of what you ultimately achieve and the type of results you get in life!

A wise man once said, "The mind is like a parachute, it works best when opened."

Expose yourself to an *enriched* and *accelerated* learning environment. *Do not get stuck or complacent in your comfort zone!* Outside your comfort zone comes confusion and chaos, but that is the very place where true learning begins.

Always begin with the end in mind. That way you are bound to have good success and a fulfilled experience.

Life is a succession of choices, so dear teenagers, make the right choices now.

To have a great harvest, one must learn to plant better thoughts and make wise choices. Just as an apple tree will not yield peaches, likewise, a poor mind-set and choices in life will not produce success.

Understand that procrastination, indecision, and a lack of knowledge are the biggest dream-killers.

Take the right decision: Is it going to be your *books* over peer pressure, moodiness, fashion, drugs, arguing with parents, etc.

Be a good student of opportunities—find and make opportunities to learn in style.

Be a great student of possibilities—think and achieve the impossible.

Be a gifted student of abilities—do not hold back, stretch, explore, and expand your mind.

Success is habitual and it leaves clues. Be a role model for up-and-coming youth. Be their blueprint.

Everyone has consummate genius within themselves. Some seem to have more than others because they are aware of it more than others are.

Society will let you get by and allow you to place less demands on yourself, but find ways to be unique in your quest for excellent grades.

Success is knocking at the door of your heart. Will you let her in, just by going that extra mile?

Secret Code for Success

S—Solo focus

U—Unique awareness of ability

C—Crystal-clear vision

C—Clarity and consistency

E—Extraordinary energy levels

S—Stop at nothing

S—Strategies—develop strategies on how you will achieve success. Or strengthen your belief . . . believe you will achieve and put the hard work in, and you will succeed.

Success costs pennies, but failure millions.

Appendix

Using the three main *learning styles* to enhance your memory.

NUMBER	PHOTOGRAPHIC (SHAPE)	AUDITORY (RHYME)	KINESTHETIC (BODY)
Zero—0	Egg/Orange	Hero	Head
One—1	Toothbrush/Pen	Sun	Neck
Two—2	Swan	Loo	Shoulders
Three—3	Camel	Tree	Bottom
Four—4	Sail of a boat	More	Folded arms
Five—5	Hook line	Hive	Fingers
Six—6	Trunk of elephant	Sinks	Earlobe
Seven—7	Cliff	Heaven	Bent leg
Eight—8	Snowman	Ate	Stomach
Nine—9	Golf club	Line	Hand-fist
Ten—10	Bat and Ball	Pen	Neck and Head

In Chapter Two—TIPS, for the acronym *I* which stands for *I*deas, we talked about linking your ideas, using funny stories, rhyming words, objects, and body parts.

Here is an example of being creative in linking your ideas. You are encouraged to link your ideas to things you already know.

Let us see how quickly we can memorize this seven-digit number **0754329.**

You can link these numbers by creating a funny story.

- The orange   0
- Rolled down the cliff   7
- And was picked up by a hook line   5

- Which, together, hit the sail of a boat   4
- And a camel   3
- A swan   2
- With a golf club saw this and laughed   9

It is very easy to create such funny stories and it has no rules. You just create something interesting or absurd and ridiculous, and this way, your memory is sure to remember any weird stories. The reason is the mind will remember vividly any emotion-packed, color-packed, or new ways to express itself.

By practicing all the time, this will become second nature.

These stories do not work only for numbers, but for any area of study you are engaged in. Start now, using your preferred learning style.

Mind Maps

A mind map is a diagram, used to represent words, ideas, tasks, or other items, linked to and arranged radially around a central key word.

A mind map can be easily created for any topic, under any subject. Let us create a mind map for the topics discussed in this book.

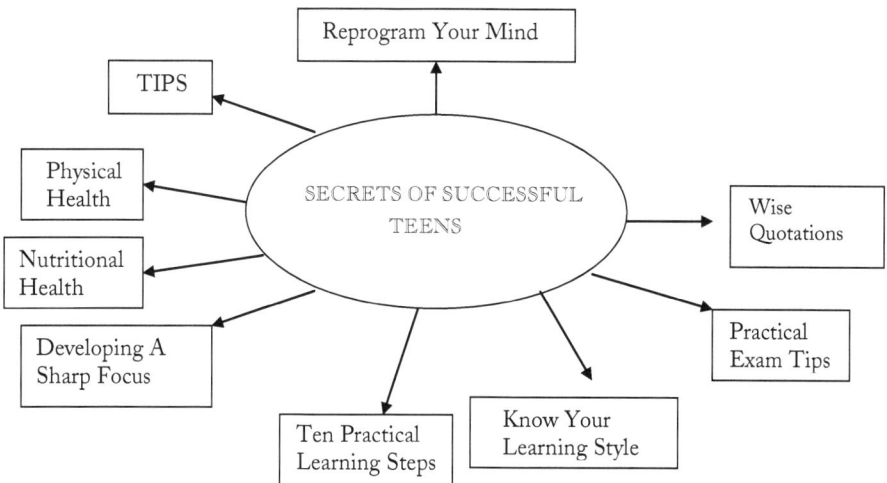

Mnemonics

Mnemonic is a memory aide or a device you can create to help in memorization. It comes in a variety of forms and is highly beneficial for memorizing in a particular order.

Mnemonics are my speciality and I encourage my students to use them as often as they can.

Examples of the usage of mnemonics in:

Spelling and Grammar-The spelling of *arithmetic* may be memorised as **A** **r**at **i**n |**T**im's **h**ome **m**ight **e**at **T**im's **i**ce **c**ream.

With the spelling of *dessert*, you can memorise that, there is *double s*, because you always want a double portion.

I always tell students with spelling difficulties to generate sub-words from words, example *believe* has a *lie* in it, likewise *tomorrow* has a name in it *Tom*, *Happen* has *pen*, *present* has *sent* to name a few.

Mathematics: In Trigonometry, we use *soh, cah, toa* to help with the calculations of *sine, cosine,* and *tangent* respectively.

Sine, which is calculated as ***O**pposite* divided by the ***H**ypotenuse*, is memorised as **SOH**.

COSINE, calculated as ADJACENT divided by the HYPOTENUSE, is memorised as **CAH**.

TANGENT, calculated as OPPOSITE divided by ADJACENT, is memorised as **TOA**.

Music: On the treble clef, we have the scales **E**very **G**ood **B**oy **D**eserves **F**avor for the notes *E, G, B, D,* and *F*.

Bible: These books in the Bible—**G**alatians, **E**phesians, **P**hilippians, and **C**olossians can be memorized as **G**o **E**at **P**op **C**orn.

Physics: To memorize the light spectrum (rainbow colors) we use *Richard Of York Gave Battle In Vain* for *Red, Orange, Yellow, Green, Blue, Indigo,* and *Violet*.

Biology: The seven life processes that all living things undergo can be memorized as:

M..................................*Movement*
R...................................*Respiration*
S....................................*Sensitivity*

G...................................*Growth*
R...................................*Reproduction*
E...................................*Excretion*
N...................................*Nutrition*

Mrs. Gren will always help you to memorize your seven life processes.

Go ahead and use this incredible memorization device to your advantage.

"The true art of memory is the art of attention."
Samuel Johnson

"We all learn best in our own ways. Some people do better studying one subject at a time, while some do better studying three things at once. Some people do best in a structured, linear way, while others do best jumping around, surrounding a subject rather than traversing it. Some people prefer to learn by manipulating models, and others by reading."
Bill Gates

All the best in your studies and in your pursuance of excellent grades.

Above all, ask God for wisdom!

Your success is my passion.

You are a success!

Other best-selling books by Laura Lyseight:

- ✓ Teens- Beat Future Economic Crisis!

An incredible exposure to the habits of the teen entrepreneur even before they are exposed to the real world. It explores what attitudes they form; knowing their attitude in certain specific areas of life is what will determine their attitude. Learn to create your business before the chains of mortgages, family responsibilities, and credit card debt lay hold of you.

- ✓ The Teen With A Millionaire Mindset

Are you wondering why people are stuck in dead-end jobs and are you worried about the economic recession? Or better yet, why have all the grown-ups you know become given-ups? All human minds are in a slumbering state until awakened for exploits. This book will help any teen discover his own unique path to make millions.

- ✓ 1001 Life Changing Quotes 4 TEENS

Words have power. Words spoken at the right time are like the taste of honey on the tongue.

As a teen, you are faced with so many challenges, and these words of wisdom will help you chart your successful route through life.

You will learn from 150 intelligent quotes on youth, 100 thought-provoking quotes on studies, health, money, entrepreneurship, as well as powerful quotes from Jesus, and lots more.

I discovered the power found in words when a suicidal teen changed her perception about life after I spoke a few words of wisdom to her. As the light lit up in her head she vowed never to be in a depressed mood again.

Printed in Great Britain
by Amazon